WILDLIFE OF ALASKA

NORTH TO ALASKA

Lynn M. Stone

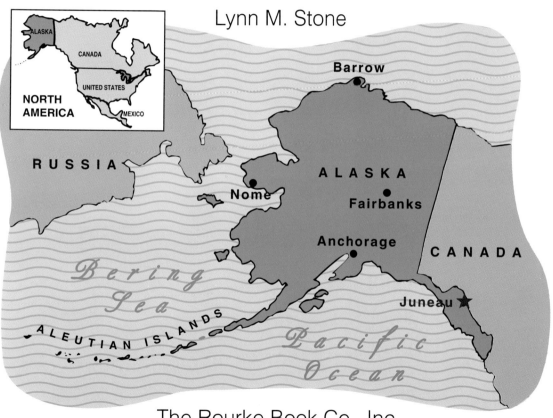

The Rourke Book Co., Inc.
Vero Beach, Florida 32964

Edited by Sandra A. Robinson

PHOTO CREDITS
All photos © Lynn M. Stone except page 4, courtesy Alaska
Division of Tourism

Library of Congress Cataloging-in-Publication Data

Stone, Lynn M.
  Wildlife of Alaska / by Lynn M. Stone.
  p. cm. — (North to Alaska)
  Includes index.
  ISBN 1-55916-026-8
  1. Zoology—Alaska—Juvenile literature. [1. Zoology—Alaska.]
I. Title. II. Series: Stone, Lynn M. North to Alaska.
QL161.S76 1994
596.09798—dc20   93-42649
                                                        CIP
Printed in the USA   AC

TABLE OF CONTENTS

WILDLIFE OF ALASKA

Alaska has a great variety of wild animals because it has a great variety of **habitats,** or animal homes.

Alaska's animals live in forests, on the treeless **tundra,** in grassy valleys, on rugged mountains, and in the lakes and seas.

Some of Alaska's animal **species,** or kinds, don't live anywhere else in the United States. These unusual animals include polar bears, Dall sheep, musk oxen and Kodiak bears. The giant Kodiak is the largest meat-eating animal on Earth.

*Dall sheep rams gather
on a sunny mountain peak*

FISH

Alaska's seas and waterways are homes for trout, pike, salmon, grayling, halibut, cod and other fish. Perhaps the most amazing fish are salmon.

Each summer adult salmon return from the sea to the freshwater streams and lakes where they were born. The fish swim against the flow of water and sometimes leap waterfalls to reach their birthplaces. After laying their eggs, the adult salmon die.

As they return to freshwater streams each summer, salmon are a favorite food of Alaska brown bears

LAND BIRDS

One of Alaska's largest land birds is the bald eagle — America's national bird. Bald eagles live along the coasts, where they build huge nests of sticks.

Another bird Alaskans know well is the ptarmigan (TAR muh gun). The chickenlike ptarmigans always match their surroundings. They have brown feathers in summer and white feathers in winter.

Mostly fish-eaters, bald eagles live throughout coastal Alaska

WATER BIRDS

Alaska's rivers, lakes and seas are perfect homes for thousands of "water birds." Each water bird has its favorite kind of water habitat, such as a marsh or a lake.

Many kinds of loons, ducks and geese nest near lakes and rivers. Puffins and oystercatchers are two of the birds that live near salt water.

Alaska's water birds range in size from the littlest, sparrow-sized sandpipers to wild swans and five-foot-tall sandhill cranes.

The unusual, chisel-shaped bill of the black oystercatcher helps it open shellfish that cling to rocky Alaskan shores

*A cousin of otters, skunks and weasels, the pine marten
hunts red squirrels in the treetops*

Snowflakes shower a wolf

MAMMALS OF THE SEA

Alaskan seas are homes for seals, sea lions, walruses, whales, porpoises and sea otters. The northern seas freeze during the winter. Polar bears, looking for seals, prowl the ice.

Most sea mammals stay warm with a layer of fat called blubber. The sea otter, though, stays warm with its very thick, soft fur.

Many sea mammals, even in Alaska, are being hurt by pollution in the oceans.

A sea otter, cradling her pup, paddles in Alaska's Kachemak Bay

MAMMALS OF THE TUNDRA

The carpet of low plants called tundra looks like a wide, treeless meadow in northern Alaska.

During the short Arctic summer, many wild animals live on the tundra. Birds nest on the tundra, and herds of **caribou** munch on tundra plants. Caribou are northern cousins of deer.

Wolves hunt caribou, Arctic hares and **lemmings** on the tundra. Arctic foxes, ground squirrels, weasels and grizzly bears live on the tundra, too.

16

A caribou bull pauses from feeding on the shrubby tundra of Alaska's interior

MAMMALS OF MEADOWS AND MARSHES

Alaska's wetlands are homes for beavers, minks and river otters. Beavers make ponds by building dams of mud and branches. The dams stop the flow of streams. The blocked water becomes a pond.

Grassy meadows next to streams and seashores are favorite hunting grounds for brown bears. Brown bears, which sometimes weigh more than 1,000 pounds, graze on grass. They also splash into streams to catch salmon.

*Giant bear of the coast,
a "brownie" lunches on a clam
it has dug from an Alaskan beach*

MAMMALS OF THE FOREST

Alaska's forests provide food and hiding places for porcupines, snowshoe rabbits, red squirrels and other animals.

Porcupines, rabbits and squirrels are plant-eaters. Other forest animals are **predators,** or hunters. They catch and eat the plant-eaters. The sleek **marten,** for example, chases red squirrels through the treetops. Wolves track moose in the forest. **Lynxes** hunt snowshoe rabbits.

Black bears are not fussy. They eat both plants and animals.

Big "snowshoe" paws of the handsome lynx help it stay on top of the snow

MAMMALS OF THE MOUNTAINS

A few hardy animals call Alaska's rugged, windy mountains home. Most mountain mammals survive by feeding on patches of grass and other low-lying plants.

When winter arrives, Dall sheep and mountain goats move downhill into more sheltered areas. Ground squirrels, **marmots** and **pikas** snuggle into their burrows. They sleep winter away in **hibernation.**

Glossary

caribou (KARE uh boo) — large, northern cousins of deer, found in large herds; wild reindeer

habitat (HAB uh tat) — the special kind of area in which an animal lives, such as mountain meadows

hibernation (hi ber NAY shun) — the sleeplike state in which certain animals survive winter

lemming (LEH ming) — a short-tailed, mouselike rodent

lynx (LINKS) — a thick-furred wildcat of the Far North; the lynx resembles a bobcat

marmot (MAR mut) — a large, burrowing ground squirrel of the western mountains of North America

marten (MART in) — a tree-climbing member of the weasel and otter family; the marten resembles a large weasel

pika (PIE kuh) — a squeaky, rat-sized animal of mountain rockslides; the pika is related to rabbits

predator (PRED uh ter) — an animal that kills other animals for food

species (SPEE sheez) — a certain kind of animal within a closely-related group, such as a *grizzly* bear

tundra (TUN druh) — the treeless carpet of low-lying plants in the Far North and on mountains above the tree line

INDEX